Rounds and Canons and Rounds and Canons and Rounds and

For Reading, Recreation and Performance

For Viola Ensemble, or with Violin and /or Cello

Composed, compiled, arranged and edited
by William Starr

ISBN 0-87487-981-7
3 5 7 9 8 6 4 2

Editor: Judi Gowe

GW00503122

CONTENTS

INTRODUCTION

How are these rounds concluded?

1. In rounds with no fermatas, the parts end one at a time. The leader indicates the number of repetitions at the beginning.

2. In rounds with fermatas, all of the parts end at the same time at the leader's signal. (All parts will be at different fermatas.)

   (a) The fermatas indicate possible stopping points only, not the duration of the final notes. The final notes may be lengthened (as with a regular fermata), or not, depending upon the character of the piece.

   (b) The fermatas are disregarded until the leader indicates the conclusion.

SOME SUGGESTIONS FOR PRACTICE AND PERFORMANCE

1. These rounds, originally published for violin choir, are not necessarily in the proper order of difficulty for the young violist. The viola teacher should look through the rounds to pick the best order for his/her students.

2. When first reading, it is helpful to play through with all parts in unison, then divide into two or three parts as needed.

3. In performance, less advanced players may play only one part repeated again and again as the others players rotate parts.

4. More advanced players may perform the easier rounds an octave higher.

5. Dynamics may be added by the leader of the first part.

6. In rounds with a long first part, the first two parts may enter together to provide harmony at the outset.

1. O How Sweet Is Our Singing

4-part

Anonymous

2. Why Doesn't My Goose?

4-part

Anonymous

3. For Health and Strength

4-part

Dutch

4. It Is Light

4-part

Anonymous

8

5. Pauper Sum Ego (I Am Poor)

3-part

Traditional Latin

Andante (♩ = ca. 80)

6. Do, Re, Mi, Fa

4-part

Traditional

Andante (♩ = ca. 80)

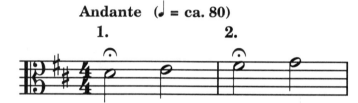

7. Hallelujah!

2-part

Boyce

Moderato (♩ = ca. 92)

8. Praise God

4-part

Tallis

*At conclusion, first part stops here.

9. Chairs to Mend

3-part

Hayes

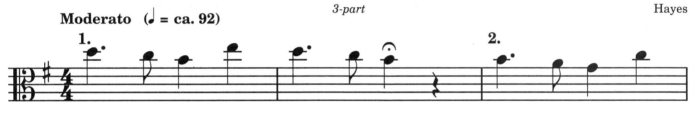

10. John Ran

4-part

Arnold

11. O How Lovely Is the Evening

3-part

Traditional

Allegretto (♩ = ca. 116)

12. Little Tom Tinker

4-part

Traditional

Andante (♩ = ca. 80)

13. Aura Lee
4-part

Poulton
Arr. Starr

Moderato ($\quad$ = ca. 92)

12

14. White Coral Bells

2-part

English

Allegretto (♩ = ca. 104)

15. Good Night to You All

3-part

Anonymous

Moderato (♩ = ca. 92)

16. Jesus, Have Mercy

3-part

Ockeghem

17. Row the Boat, Whittington

3-part

Anonymous

18. Alleluia

3-part

Mozart

14

19. Dona Nobis Pacem

3-part

Anonymous

20. Sue and John Are Friends

4-part

Starr

21. Shalom

4-part

Jewish Folk Song

*At conclusion, first part stops here.

22. The Scale

3-part

Beethoven

Allegretto (♩ = ca. 104)

23. Come With Me

3-part

Starr

Andante (♩ = ca. 88)

24. Hallelujah!

3-part

Jewish Folk Song
Arr. Starr

25. Peacc to You

4-part

Starr

26. Vigoroso
5-part

Starr

27. Swaying Song
4-part

Starr

28. Come, Follow

3-part

Traditional

29. ”Tis Women

4-part

Purcell

30. Gossip Round
4-part

Anonymous

31. First Commandment
3-part

Haydn

These are four separate rounds. If all are to be played consecutively in performance, it is suggested that each round be played only once in its complete 3-part version. Players could then alternate playing the first parts of each round.

32. Haste Thee, Nymph

3-part

Arnold

33. Long Live the Queen
4-part

Boyce

34. Run, Susie, Run
4-part

Starr

35. Lullaby for Suzanne
5-part

Starr

36. Fie, Nay Prithee
3-part

Purcell

37. Give Thanks to the Lord

4-part

Starr

Since the 1st part is quite long, it is suggested that in performance the 1st and 2nd parts enter together to provide instant harmony.

38. Tzena, Tzena
3-part

Jewish Folk Song

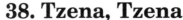

Allegretto (♩ = ca. 112)

39. Hatikvah (Hope)
4-part

Jewish Folk Song
Arr. Starr

Andante (♩ = ca. 72)

40. Run, Martina
4-part

Starr

Allegretto (♩ = ca. 100)

41. Sadness

4-part

Starr

42. All Welcome Now the Lovely May

3-part

Schubert

43. Alleluia

4-part

Hayes

44. Si Contemo

3-part

Caldara

45. Two Grenadiers

4-part

Schumann
Arr. Starr

46. Martina Playing
4-part

Starr

Moderato (♩ = ca. 96)

47. Amazing Grace
4-part

American
Arr. Starr

Since the 1st part is quite long, it is suggested that in performance the 1st and 2nd parts enter together to provide instant harmony.

Slowly (♩ = ca. 72)

48. Hey Ho

3-part

Melville

Adagio (♩ = ca. 69)

*At conclusion, first part stops here.

49. Witches' Dance

4-part

Paganini
Arr. Starr

50. Wake Up, Sleepy Head!

4-part

C. Starr

With spirit (♩. = ca. 88)

51. Come Swing With Me
4-part

Starr

52. The Goblin
4-part

Haydn

53. Happy-go-lucky
4-part

C. Starr
Arr. W. Starr

54. Phoebus and Her Son
4-part

Haydn

55. Skip to My Lou

4-part

Arr. Starr

56. Turk Was a Faithful Dog
4-part

Haydn

57. Sleep, Baby, Sleep
4-part

Brahms

*At conclusion, first part stops here.

58. If I Know What You Know
3-part

Anonymous

59. Lacrimoso (Lament)
4-part

Mozart

60. Tick, Tock

Andante (♩ = ca. 80)

4-part

Beethoven

61. Andante

(♩ = ca. 76)

3-part

Mozart

38

62. Get Ready to Go
4-part

Mozart

64. Love of Knowledge
4-part

Haydn

65. Ave Maria
3-part

Beethoven

66. Alleluia
4-part

Mozart

Andante (= ca. 88)

67. Start Playing
3-part

Starr

Andante (= ca. 80)

cresc.

f

dim.

*At conclusion, first part stops here.

68. Adagio

6-part

Beethoven

42

69. Do, Re, Mi, Fa, Sol

4-part

Starr

70. Kyrie

5-part

Mozart

71. 'Tis So, 'Tis Not
4-part

Starr

72. Sanctus
5-part

Clemens

73. Cleverness

4-part

Haydn

Moderato (♩ = ca. 88)

This page has been left blank to facilitate page turns.

74. A Little Blues

4-part

Starr

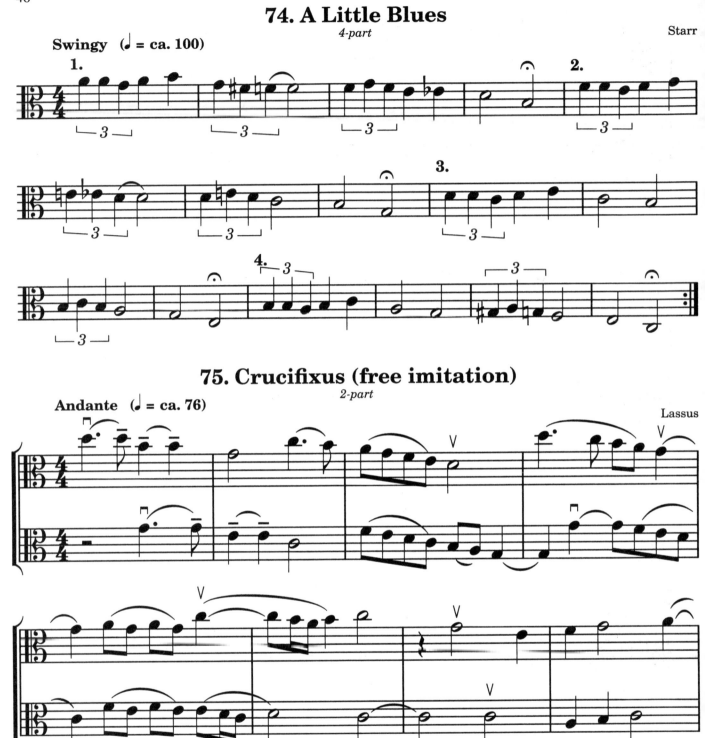

75. Crucifixus (free imitation)

2-part

Lassus

76. O How Softly
4-part

Brahms

Note that the 1st and 2nd parts are inversions of the 3rd and 4th parts!
All parts enter as written. Use the fermatas after the repeat.

77. Pleni Sunt Coeli (Canon)

3-part

Palestrina

All parts enter as written. The dynamic suggestions are for clarity in performance.

78. Canon in D

3-part

Telemann

All parts enter as written. Use the fermatas after the repeat.

Allegretto (♩ = ca. 96)

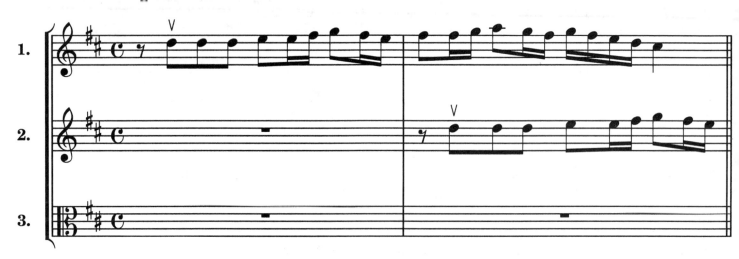

79. Tandem Waltz (Canon)

2-part

Starr

80. The Chase (Canon)

2-part

Starr